*To our dad and grandfather, Don Clifton,
who understood that every child has the
potential to be a great bucket filler
Mary and Tom*

*To my mother, Ginger
Maurie*

GALLUP PRESS
1251 Avenue of the Americas
23rd Floor
New York, NY 10020

Library of Congress Control Number: 2008944304
ISBN: 978-1-59562-027-9

First Printing: 2009
10 9 8

Printed in Canada

HOW FULL
IS YOUR
BUCKET?
For Kids

Written by
Tom Rath and Mary Reckmeyer

Illustrated by
Maurie J. Manning

Felix was putting one of the last blocks on his tower when his little sister came in. "I want to build with you," she said. Felix scowled, "Go away. You're too little."

THWACK!

Grandpa!

Grandpa shook his head.

"Felix, you just dipped from your sister's bucket."

"Like everyone else, Anna has an invisible bucket. When it's empty, she feels bad. But when it's full, she feels great. Didn't you ever notice your own bucket?"

"Invisible bucket?" Hmmm...sometimes Felix couldn't quite tell when his grandfather was joking.

But the next morning when Felix woke up, there it was —
a small gray bucket floating above his head.

When Felix came down to have breakfast, his mom was in a hurry.

"I've got a meeting this morning —
and it's almost time to go."

"Anna, sit still!"

Felix slipped, and Choco Wheats scattered across the floor.

"Felix!" yelled his mom. "You should have used the stool to reach that!"

Felix could feel his bucket tip and big invisible drips spill out…

Drip. Drip.

"Ha Ha!!" Anna laughed as she crunched the cereal with her shoe.

Drip.

"Get the broom and clean that up before you miss the bus," scolded Mom.

With the school bus honking, Felix quickly swept up the Choco Wheats and grabbed the last blueberry muffin. But before he could even take one bite…

...Buster jumped up and grabbed the muffin from his hand.

Drip.

Hey, look at Felix's new backpack! My baby brother has one just like it!

Drip.

It was still morning, and Felix's bucket felt almost empty.

As he watched his classmates walk into the room, he secretly hoped they would trip and fall.

That's what it feels like when you have an empty bucket.

Felix slumped into his seat and waited for something else bad to happen.

Mrs. Bumblenickel walked slowly up to his desk and handed him a paper.
He could hardly bear to look…

Felix, you wrote a wonderful story.
Would you please share it with the class?

Felix grinned and felt a big
drop land right in his bucket.

Drop!

The class grew quiet. They laughed at all the right places and "oohed" at the scary parts.

When Felix finally read, "The End," everyone clapped — even Emily, who sat next to him and didn't usually like dinosaurs.

Felix felt a whole shower of drops land in his bucket. Maybe the day wouldn't be so bad after all.

Drop!

Drop!

By afternoon, Felix's bucket was nearly full.

At recess when he looked around, Felix suddenly realized that his grandpa was right — everyone else had a bucket too!

The strange thing was that for every drop he helped put in someone else's bucket, he felt another drop in his own bucket.

When Felix burst in the door after school, he shouted, "You were right Grandpa! I DO have a bucket, and I understand how it works!"

Then he saw Anna's torn doll.

"Bad dog!" he almost scolded.

But then he thought — dogs might have invisible buckets too.

"Your doll will be okay, Anna," said Felix.

"Mom will fix her..."

"...until then, do you want to help me build the tallest building in the world with my blocks?"

And so they did.